SLAM!™
STARS OF WRESTLING

KOFI KINGSTON
CHAMP OF SMACKDOWN

D0125921

BRIDGET HEOS

rosen publishing's
rosen central®

New York

For three of my favorite baby faces and Celtics fans—Justin, Johnny, and Richie Heos

Published in 2012 by The Rosen Publishing Group, Inc.
29 East 21st Street, New York, NY 10010

Library of Congress Cataloging-in-Publication Data

Heos, Bridget.
Kofi Kingston: champ of smackdown/Bridget Heos.—1st ed.
       p. cm.—(Slam! stars of wrestling)
Includes bibliographical references and index.
ISBN 978-1-4488-5535-3 (library binding)—
ISBN 978-1-4488-5595-7 (pbk.)—
ISBN 978-1-4488-5596-4 (6-pack)
1. Kingston, Kofi, 1981—Juvenile literature. 2. Wrestlers—United States—Biography—Juvenile literature. I. Title.
GV1196.K62H46 2012
796.812092—dc23
[B]
                                                                    2011023329

Manufactured in the United States of America

CPSIA Compliance Information: Batch #W12YA: For further information, contact Rosen Publishing, New York, New York, at 1-800-237-9932.

CONTENTS

INTRODUCTION

Kofi Kingston had had it with the bully Randy Orton. Kicking a legend like Rowdy Roddy Piper while he was down? Who did he think he was? Kofi knew exactly what Orton was: dead meat. He charged the ring and blindsided Orton. The battle quickly spilled out of the ring and onto the concrete floor. There, an enraged Orton attacked Kingston. The usually happy-go-lucky Ghanian slammed into the cold metal. This meant war.

Nearing the roaring fans, Kofi put Orton in a headlock and muscled him over to the announcers' table. Luckily, the dumbfounded announcers were seated at a different table. Kofi grasped for the nearest thing he could find: a metal box lid. He wielded it like a shield against Orton. Soon, Orton lay unmoving on the table. Kofi didn't give him the chance to wake up. The lights were out, and it was time for bed.

Kofi climbed onto the metal railing that separated the fans from the floor. As his theme song, "S.O.S.," played, he lifted his arms and sang, "Boom, boom."

Kofi Kingston wrestles Chuck Palumbo at WWE SmackDown in Sydney, Australia, in 2008. Palumbo, weighing in at around 280 pounds (127 kg), outweighs Kofi by around 60 pounds (27 kg).

Then he leapt high in the air, his legs in front of him, poised for his signature boom drop.

The crowd went wild. But the announcers were baffled. What had happened to the perpetually smiling Kofi? Randy Orton had happened to him. He stood for the kind of bully Kofi had never suffered—even from his first time on a televised wrestling event. But would the bullied become the bully? Would Kofi become a heel? Or would he become a more serious "baby face," the deceptively innocent name for wrestling's greatest heroes.

This is the story of how a small, nice guy became one of wrestling's most athletic, scrappy, and worthy opponents.

1 SMALL BUT MIGHTY

Born on August 14, 1981, in Ghana, West Africa, Kofi Sarkodie-Mensah was the son of scholars. His mother and father moved the family to America when Kofi was a toddler. They hoped to get jobs at a university. His mother, Elizabeth, became an anthropologist, and his father, Kwasi, became the head of reference at the O'Neill Library at Boston College. Little did they know that Kofi would soon discover his dream job by watching Saturday morning television.

Kofi's family lived in Winchester, an affluent Boston suburb. However, Kofi describes his neighborhood as "the pits," a not-so-wealthy part of town. Kofi attended public school, and on Saturdays he studied wrestling moves by watching WWE on television. He began watching wrestling in the late 1980s but mainly remembers the wrestlers of the 1990s. He liked Ricky "the Dragon" Steamboat for his high-flying moves and martial arts. He watched Bret and Owen Hart. He told the *Mirror* on April 22, 2009, "I loved to hate Owen Hart." Seeing him act like he'd won a match when it had only just begun, he'd think, "This guy. Who does he think he is?"

Kofi always wanted to go to a live WWE event—or at least watch a pay-per-view matchup, but it was too expensive. So he would create his own wrestling matches. Every wrestler has a rival. Kofi's was a Bugs Bunny doll! It had wire limbs so that he could shape it—a fun feature for tying an opponent in knots in the wrestling ring.

Kofi was a good athlete. He played basketball and idolized Boston Celtics star Larry Bird. He played football, too. However, he felt limited by his

Kofi Kingston's mother and father immigrated to the United States from Ghana. This photo of a busy market in Accra, Ghana, was taken in 1985, soon after Kofi's family moved to America.

size. Going into high school, he weighed only about 95 pounds (43 kilograms). As a wrestler, he could compete against students his size—103 pounds (46 kg) or less. He joined the team. The wrestling he knew from watching television was more glitzy and bombastic than the high school sport. Still, he felt like he had found his ideal competition. Wrestlers have to be quick on their feet and good at pinning opponents using upper body strength. Kofi was both. He became a high school star.

Kofi grew in high school and eventually wrestled at 125 pounds (56 kg). At that point, he accidentally broke an opponent's leg during an arm drag. The injured young man, Tom Mello, didn't get mad at Kofi. Later, he told the *Boston Globe* in 2009, "Kofi is the most kind-hearted person I've ever met, constantly smiling."

Kofi didn't win every match, but he was in the upper echelon of high school wrestlers. His senior year, he got fourth at state. His mother went to every match and was proud of her son, especially because he was growing up to be a nice young man. Kofi loved wrestling, but when it came time to choose a path after high school, he did what he thought he was supposed to do. He went to college to prepare for an office job. He studied communications at Boston College. Rather than wrestling, he was in a step group, which is a style of dancing involving clapping and stomping.

All the while, he hoped to get a job that allowed him to earn a good living. Deep down, he knew an

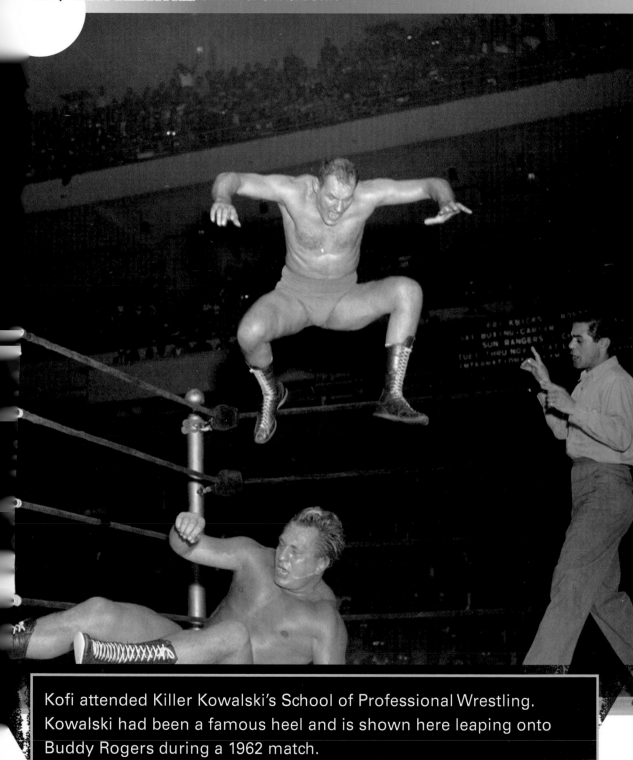

Kofi attended Killer Kowalski's School of Professional Wrestling. Kowalski had been a famous heel and is shown here leaping onto Buddy Rogers during a 1962 match.

office job wouldn't be the right fit for him. Still, after college, he joined the Staples advertising team. After a year of working in a cubicle, he felt like he needed a change. That's when he remembered his Saturdays watching wrestling. That's when he remembered his dream.

Kofi, Chaos, and Killers

In 2005, Kofi returned to wrestling. He invested money he had gotten from a tax return to train at Chaotic Wrestling in North Andover, Massachusetts. Chaotic Wrestling is a small New England promotion. In wrestling, a promotion is a company of wrestlers that performs for audiences. Local promotions, also known as indy wrestling, were common in the early days of wrestling. Then, in the 1980s and 1990s, many local wrestlers were recruited to WWE (at the time called WWF.) Other local promotions were bought out. However, some local promotions remain and others are just getting started.

Chaotic is also home of Killer Kowalski's School of Professional Wrestling. Killer Kowalski was a professional wrestler from 1947–1977, and for a while, the most hated heel in the game. After retiring, his good guy qualities came to light as he worked to raise money for children with special needs. His wrestling school also became famous, as it was the training ground for Triple H. Mike Hollow was Kofi's teacher at Killer Kowalski's School. As Triple H's former trainer, he is known to teach WWE-style wrestling.

Some young people might be surprised that there are schools for professional wrestlers. Here is what training is like today at the Killer Kowalski School: students take three classes per week—5:45 to 9:00 PM Tuesdays and Thursdays, and Saturday 10:00 AM to noon. Similar to grade school or high school, students bring a notebook and take detailed notes on the moves they are learning. These notebooks are graded by their teachers.

CHOOSING A WRESTLING SCHOOL

If you are interested in attending wrestling school, here are some questions to ask:

- How much emphasis is placed on safety and what is the safety record of the school?

  People have lost their lives or suffered serious injuries while wrestling. Safety should be the top priority of any school.
- What are the tuition and fees?

  Wrestling school can be expensive. Make sure you know the costs up front.
- What wrestlers have graduated from your school?

  A school with graduates who are now professional wrestlers illustrates good training and a solid reputation.
- Will I have opportunities to wrestle in events?

  This is good practice and can help you build a reputation as a wrestler.
- How old do students have to be?

  Nowadays, many school require students to be eighteen, but some allow children as young as thirteen to enroll. Keep in mind that your high school wrestling team may be free or inexpensive to join. This can be good training for pro wrestling as well.

Before students can have a match, they have to know the fundamentals: moves, taking bumps, ring position, and timing. In addition, students learn how to create a persona. They can choose to be a heel (bad guy) or face (good guy). The rule is, when they are in the ring they have to be in character, which is good practice for real life. Finally, students learn the importance of respecting themselves, others, and professional wrestling.

Because the school is owned by Chaotic Wrestling, students get to participate in shows as writers, wrestlers, producers, referees, and more. Using his college and corporate background in advertising, Kofi thought about how he wanted to market himself as a Chaotic wrestler. During the long commute from work to wrestling school and home again, he often listened to reggae. One night, in the gym, he started talking in a Jamaican accent. His fellow wrestlers encouraged him to develop that character.

Soon, he was making promo videos as Kofi Nahaje Kingston, an angry Jamaican. In one, he stands in front of a demolished building and asks Americans if this is the best they can do. He says, "Kofi Nahaje Kingston will rebuild Chaotic Wrestling, the first step in rebuilding this pathetic nation." He was paying homage

Ricky "the Dragon" Steamboat, shown here wrestling Don "Magnificent" Muraco in 1985, was one of Kofi's favorite wrestlers growing up. Like Steamboat, Kofi is a high–flyer, or a wrestler known for aerial moves.

WRESTLERS KOFI WATCHED ON TELEVISION

- **Bret Hart** Born in Calgary, Canada, Bret Hart wrestled in his father's Stampede Wrestling promotion. He worked his way up to WWE, winning several championships, including matches against his brother Owen.
- **Ricky "the Dragon" Steamboat** A native of Honolulu, Hawaii, Ricky "the Dragon" Steamboat took WWE by storm in 1985 with his fire-breathing pre-game stunts and high-flying attacks. He now works behind the scenes for WWE.
- **Junkyard Dog** Hailing from Charlotte, North Carolina, Junkyard spent much of his time wrestling in southern promotions. While in WWF, he was extremely popular with kids. He had his own action figure, was featured on TV shows, and sang his own theme song, "Grab Them Cakes."

to Ludvig Borgden, a Norwegian wrestler who went up against All-American Lex Luger and was famous for his anti-American rhetoric. This persona would be the foundation for a more lighthearted Jamaican persona. Soon, he would drop the Nahaje—and some of the anger.

Kofi worked various local promotions—all in hopes of making it to WWE. This is typical of wrestlers just starting out. They may try out for development training regions, such as Florida Championship Wrestling. (This can cost $1,000!) Also, they might make connections through their coaches, managers, or agents. Like other entertainment fields, it is rare to make it as a professional wrestler. It takes a combination of talent, dedication, and luck. As it turned out, Kofi had all three.

2 TROUBLE IN PARADISE

In August 2006, WWE visited the Chaotic Wrestling Training Center for an open tryout—the first ever held at the school. About twenty wrestlers showed up, all hoping for a contract. The WWE chose Kofi! He would be part of the WWE Developmental Federation. Similar to minor league baseball, the Developmental Federation is training ground for WWE wrestlers. The wrestlers perform in smaller markets or before main events, and the matches are occasionally televised.

Kofi wrestled for Deep South and Ohio Valley Wrestling, which at the time were developmental territories. He also wrestled for Florida Championship Wrestling, still a developmental territory for WWE. While working these promotions, Kofi met other wrestlers such as CM Punk and Dashing Cody Rhodes. He developed moves like the boom drop and Jamaican Buzz Saw (now Trouble in Paradise.) He practiced tag team matches. He also got to go up against WWE main roster wrestlers during dark (untelevised) matches.

Kofi's last stop on the training circuit was ECW (Extreme Championship Wrestling). ECW had been an independent production, with many stars getting their start there. WWE acquired it in 2003 as its third brand and, for some young wrestlers, a final stop before being drafted to Raw or SmackDown. It aired on the SyFy channel. WWE dropped ECW in February 2010.

While a member of ECW, Kofi retained his Jamaican persona, thinking people would be more familiar with the nearby island than his birth country

of Ghana. Only instead of being an angry Jamaican, now he was a happy-go-lucky Jamaican. Instead of being a heel, he was a face.

By the end of 2007, ECW was airing promo videos for Kofi during televised wrestling events. The videos show him on a beach in Jamaica. When he sees a man steal something off a beach towel, he says, "Looks like there's trouble in paradise." Then loud noises are heard as women and children look on. At last, Kofi emerges with the loot, having dealt with the troublemaker. In another video, Kofi stands up for a man who is being bullied by another man.

Beyond being the "first Jamaican WWE wrestler," Kofi wanted to present fresh moves and a fresh persona. In the videos, Kofi had revealed an important part of his persona: just because he was happy-go-lucky didn't mean he would let bad guys do bad stuff. Not

Mark Henry, who weighs in at 398 pounds (181 kg) and stands 6' 4" (1.93 m), tosses Kofi Kingston onto a ladder during the Money in the Bank Ladder Match at WrestleMania XXV in 2009.

on his watch. This characteristic would be important in his later feud with Randy Orton.

On January 22, 2008, Kofi's moment had arrived. It was his television wrestling debut for ECW on the SyFy channel. The announcers introduced him as the first Jamaican wrestler. He faced David Owen from North Carolina, who weighed in at 250 pounds (113 kg). Kofi weighed just 218 pounds (99 kg). Luckily for Kofi, Owen was a "jobber," a wrestler who routinely loses matches. Jobbers are used in debut matches to make newcomers look good.

High-Flying Kofi

Kofi entered the ring wearing the colors of the Jamaican flag—black, yellow and green—and to the theme song "S.O.S." Moments into the match, Kofi did a sweep (which is like a slide tackle) that brought both him and Owen to their knees. Afterward, Kofi hopped up like he had springs in his feet. One announcer said, "Kofi Kingston bounces right back up with a smile on his face. You got to love a guy who smiles in the middle of a fight."

After taking a few blows from Owen, Kofi cornered the bald, tattooed opponent. With a back somersault, he tossed Owen behind him. This move, called a monkey flip, seriously diminished Owen's resolve. He was losing strength. He did manage to put Kofi in a solid headlock, but Kofi broke free. The next time Owen lunged at Kofi, Kofi leapt completely over him. He jumped again and took Owen down.

The announcers said they hoped WWE veterans were taking notes. Kofi was bringing an offense and confidence they'd never seen before. After a classic flapjack (in which Kofi lifted Owen by the knees and threw him, so that he landed flat on his stomach), it was time to show Owen his signature move: the boom drop. Kofi stood over Owen and said, "Boom, boom." Then

During Kofi's debut, WWE announcers praised him for doing moves audiences had never seen, such as this jump kick move against Matt Hardy on June 13, 2009.

he leapt in the air, his legs straight out in front of him, and landed on Owen like he was a trampoline. As if that wasn't enough, Kofi showed Owen his finisher. As Owen stood up, Kofi did a jumping roundhouse kick—the Jamaican Buzz Saw. Finally, he pinned Owen.

After the match, the announcers noted how difficult it was to come up with a move the world had never seen before. Yet Kofi had come up with three or four. He had just made his debut and already he was a rising star.

But later that year, Kofi faced controversy. A July 2, 2008, BBC *Focus on Africa* magazine article revealed that he was not from Jamaica but Ghana. The reporter asked why Kofi was denying his African birthplace? To make matters worse, the reporter quoted Kofi's mother as saying that his cousins in Africa were asking the same question. The article said that Kofi had since asked his family to stop talking to the media. A quote from Kofi said of his mother, "She's very happy I am doing what I want to do … But I don't think she knows how big wrestling really is."

The controversy wasn't exactly devastating to Kofi's career or family life. Kofi has always been close to his mother—she attends Boston matches and is a good sport when heels talk trash to her from inside the ring. Also, all wrestlers have

AMERICAN PRO WRESTLING: A BOMBASTIC HISTORY

In the early 1900s, professional wrestling was a competitive sport, much like boxing. Then, in the 1920s, promoters began scripting the matches. But they didn't tell the fans! Fans eventually caught on but still thought wrestling was entertaining. Jim Londos was the first "face" in pro wrestling. Nicknamed the Golden Greek, he showed that a persona was good for business. More "faces"—usually young, handsome guys, and "heels," typically older and overweight, were introduced.

Needing to fill arenas during the 1930s, promoters created a more circuslike atmosphere. Wrestlers had over-the-top gimmicks and moves. In the 1950s, wrestling was promoted on television to draw fans to live, local events. These local promotions gave rise to

Pro wrestling permeated 1980s pop culture. Wrestlers such as Hulk Hogan (*right*), pictured here with actor and pop icon–turned–wrestler Mr. T, appeared on *Saturday Night Live* episodes, such as this one airing March 30, 1985.

wrestlers who became national sensations. WWWF, the precursor to WWF and then WWE, was created in 1963. Once it was broadcast on cable television, wrestling became big business.

By the 1980s, wrestlers were hosting *Saturday Night Live*, being interviewed by news magazines, and being made into action figures. In the 1990s, Monday Night Wrestling Wars pitted WWF against WCW for ratings. Eventually, WCW was sold to WWF. Now known as WWE, it dominates the world wrestling scene, though TNA (Total Nonstop Action) is making headway as a televised promotion.

personas, so it wasn't big news that Kofi was Ghanian and not Jamaican. (In fact, adopting a nationality as part of a wrestling persona has gone on since the earliest days of scripted wrestling in America.) However, Kofi eventually dropped the Jamaican persona and began to be introduced as a wrestler from Ghana. This allowed him to become more two-dimensional. He was still a "baby face" and a good-natured guy. But even the most laid-back person can't like everybody. For, Kofi, that somebody would soon be Randy Orton.

3 KING OF THE BOOM DROP

Today, Raw and SmackDown are the two WWE brands. Each year, a live draft allows the brands to win talent from the opposing brands. Wrestlers from two different brands compete. Whoever wins the match earns a draft pick for their brand.

In 2008, ECW was also a WWE brand that participated in the draft, and Kofi was on the roster. June 23, 2008, was a big night for all wrestlers and for Kofi in particular. The draft was being broadcast from the AT&T Center in San Antonio, Texas, to viewers around the world. Vince McMahon, CEO of WWE, was giving away $1 million of his own money to television viewers! Kofi, as part of the ECW brand, went up against John Bradshaw Layfield, known as JBL, a millionaire cowboy who wrestled for the Raw brand. If Kofi won, he would earn a draft pick for ECW. If JBL won, he would earn one for Raw. This was also an opportunity for Kofi to demonstrate to all the brands that he was ready for the big time.

JBL arrived in a limousine wearing a cowboy hat. At the start of the match, he beat up on Kofi. The announcers said JBL was treating Kofi as if he owed the cowboy money. Kofi bounced back and put the boom drop on JBL. But moments later, JBL managed to bear hug Kofi. Far from a teddy bear move, the bear hug wears down wrestlers. Veterans like JBL use it against younger, faster opponents in order to capitalize on strength over quickness.

Viewers tuned in as Vince McMahon gave away $1 million of his own money at Million Dollar Mania. Wrestlers Triple H and John Cena, and diva Maria are visible behind him at this 2008 press conference.

Fortunately for Kofi, the move backfired on JBL. Kofi broke free, and JBL was the one who was tired. Kofi began orchestrating his finish: a vertical leap onto the ropes, cornering JBL, then back to center stage for Trouble in Paradise. Kofi pinned JBL, but he managed to kick out. Kofi climbed onto the ropes for a flying body slam but missed! He did a belly flop instead. JBL pinned him. Had Kofi also missed his chance at getting drafted by Raw?

While Kofi wasn't drafted in the television draft, he was drafted in the supplemental draft, as number 28—the last draftee. He was joining well-known wrestlers such as Rey Mysterio, Batista, and Kane and fellow up-and-comer CM Punk, who would become his tag team partner.

On the Raw roster, his first match was against Chris Jericho, former Intercontinental Champion. A longtime wrestler, Jericho is currently a heel who uses his large vocabulary to insult opponents and fans alike. On June

ROWDY RODDY PIPER

Rowdy Roddy Piper was a 1980s heel who did everything from managing to wrestling to running an in-ring talk show. Far from an Oprah-type production, *Piper's Pit* guests often had the microphone yanked from their hands or were physically attacked for no reason. As a heel, Piper's bodyguard was Randy Orton's father, Cowboy Bob Orton. Piper later turned face, which put him at odds with the senior Orton. He continues to be involved with wrestling and won the World Tag Team Championship with Ric Flair as recently as 2006.

29, 2008, Jericho's rival Shawn Michaels supposedly was out of the building because of an eye injury inflicted by Jericho. But while Jericho performed the Walls of Jericho on Kofi, he caught Michaels out of the corner of his eye. Distracted, he released Kofi, who then delivered his Trouble in Paradise kick. Kofi then pinned Jericho.

The next night, they faced a mandatory rematch due to the interference. That night, Kofi won due to Jericho being disqualified (for pulling on Kofi's tights). Kofi was again Intercontinental Champion. Unfortunately, he lost the title during a Summer Slam winner-take-all-match, where he was paired with women's champion Mickie James to battle Beth Phoenix and Santino Marella.

Kofi would take on a new tag team partner. The partnership started on September 7, 2008, at Unforgiven. Backstage, CM Punk was being interviewed about defending his heavyweight championship belt. An apparently injured Randy Orton got in his face, calling him a fluke. Moments later the tag team of Cody Rhodes and Ted DiBiase, along with Manu, ambushed CM Punk. Kofi came to Punk's defense. Kofi and Punk both wound up knocked out, but a camaraderie had formed. So had Kofi's brewing hatred of Randy Orton, whom he considered a bully that needed to be put in his place.

Don't Mess with Kofi!

There are many heels that fans love to hate. Randy Orton is more of a heel that fans hate to love. Intense, earnest, and brooding, he is as hardworking and talented as he is mean. That earns him some level of respect from fans. Orton has a tentative alliance with DiBiase and Rhodes, known as Legacy, because both of their fathers were wrestlers. (Actually, so

Randy Orton, standing on the ropes above Batista and Sheamus on May 5, 2010, was the heel in one of Kofi's most popular feuds.

was Orton's father.) Punk, meanwhile, was a young face known for his straight-edged personality. Starting out as a backyard wrestler, he had worked his way through the indy wrestling ranks. He wrestled for ECW with Kofi. Like Kofi, he was known for his high-energy wrestling style.

Later that year, Kofi and Punk defeated Ted DiBiase and Cody Rhodes. They eventually lost their World Tag Team Championship to John Morrison and the Miz. Still they had become friends. Outside of the ring CM Punk and Kofi traveled together. They were the homebodies on the circuit, preferring to watch wrestling and play video games to going out. On the other hand, Kofi's animosity toward Orton would become all-out war.

SMACKDOWN VS. RAW

Among wrestling fans, SmackDown and Raw have different reputations. Raw relies on wrestling veterans such as Orton and John Cena and their longstanding rivalries. SmackDown mixes new talent with old. Raw is considered to be the more story-driven wrestling program, whereas SmackDown focuses on wrestling. Both brands are owned by WWE, and the draft is meant to mix up the rosters each year. There are sometimes team matches pitting SmackDown against Raw wrestlers. There is also a video game called *WWE SmackDown vs. Raw*, which features wrestlers from both brands.

During the October 25, 2009, WWE Championship match between Randy Orton and John Cena, Cody Rhodes and Ted DiBiase came to Orton's defense. Kofi also ran into the ring and chased Rhodes and DiBiase out of the arena. Orton lost and blamed Kofi. The next night, Kofi interrupted— via video—a rematch Orton was trying to arrange with John Cena. Kofi told Orton that he lost and nobody cared what he said now. Orton told Kofi to say it to his face.

Kofi surprised Orton by saying that he already was saying it to his face— the portrait Orton had painted on his car. Orton then watched in horror as Kofi poured paint on the car. (This was of course staged, as car vandalism is a major offense.) The performance showed management and fans that Kofi was not only an exciting wrestler, but also had good microphone skills. In other words, he could talk trash.

Rowdy Roddy Piper pummels Chris Jericho during WrestleMania XXV in 2009. Piper wrestled professionally from 1973 to 1987 but still returns to the ring on occasion.

The feud with Orton allowed Kofi to show a darker side. After all, even nice guys can't always fight with a smile on their face. On November 16, 2009, the feud between Orton and Kofi came to a head. A wrestling legend, Rowdy Roddy Piper, had challenged Orton to a street fight at Madison Square Garden in New York. (Cowboy Bob Orton and Piper had been enemies in the 1980s.) Piper arrived in street clothes: jeans and a T-shirt. While still on the mic, Orton arrived in full wrestling gear and cheap-shotted Piper. Piper fell to the ground. Out of nowhere, Kofi ran into the ring and attacked Orton. That's when the scene described in the introduction occurred.

Later, Kofi would say that defending a legend like Piper was a huge thrill. He had watched him as a kid.

Having proved that he could go head-to-head with a villain like Orton, Kofi continued to show his athleticism. He didn't win every match, but he was always entertaining. And soon, he would take his show to SmackDown.

4 A LEGENDARY OPPONENT

While Kofi didn't win every match, he was always entertaining. He proved this on March 28, 2010, during the WrestleMania XXVI Money in the Bank Ladder Match. In this match, several wrestlers battle for money in a briefcase dangled high overhead. They each get a ladder, which they climb to reach the money. They can also hit each other with the ladders. Midway through the match, Kane broke a ladder in half while battling Dolph Zigler. Kofi, recovered from an early knockout, climbed back in the ring. Kofi kicked Kane with a Trouble in Paradise. With Zigler and Kane out of the ring, Kofi had a shot at the briefcase. But the only ladder in the ring was the one Kane had broken in half! Kofi shocked the audience by walking across the ring on the two broken ladder halves, using them as stilts. Just as he was climbing the stilts to the briefcase, an old rival appeared: Drew McIntyre. Kofi lost one of the ladder stilts but tried to climb the other as it seemingly balanced on air. McIntyre pushed the ladder half, with Kofi on it, down. Eventually, the heel Jack Swagger won the ladder match. However, Kofi had earned the reputation as the most acrobatic wrestler—and one of the most athletic wrestlers—in WWE.

He is also one of the most creative, feeding his mind with tales of titans and feats of strength. Fodder for his imagination includes: superheroes, comic books (his favorites being Thor and Spiderman), Japanimation, and Saturday morning cartoons. Kofi understands that wrestling is part of a larger culture of heroism and villainy. He also understands that wrestlers—

During the WrestleMania XXVI Money in the Bank Ladder Match on March 28, 2010, Kofi used two sides of a broken ladder as stilts. He lost the match but gained the respect of the crowd.

though they are real people—have to appear capable of superhuman feats. While he eats what he likes (in Boston, his favorite is Mexican restaurant Anna's Taqueria), he exercises daily and practices hard.

On April 26, 2010, Kofi was drafted to SmackDown. Once again, his first match was against Chris Jericho. Though the two may look like bitter rivals in the ring, Kofi has said that Jericho is one of his favorite opponents. When Kofi was a nervous rookie, Jericho showed him how to have fun in the ring. Kofi realized he needed to enjoy wrestling while he could, considering the sometimes fickle nature of the business. He could rise today only to fall tomorrow.

His next match was against Christian, a heel, in a tournament for the Intercontinental Championship. Though scripted, winning this is good for a wrestler's career. The title had been stripped from Drew McIntyre, the so-called Chosen One, earlier in the year by a manager named Theodore Long. This was after McIntyre ruthlessly attacked Matt Hardy.

Kofi won the match against Christian! However, McIntyre surprised audiences by entering the ring with a letter from WWE CEO Vince McMahon. It said that Long shouldn't have suspended McIntyre. The Chosen One was renamed Intercontinental Champion. Kofi regained the championship belt in a late May match with McIntyre at Over the Limit. But by now, McIntyre was obsessed with regaining the belt and showing Long that he was wrong for ever taking it away. A new feud for Kofi was underway.

Home Sweet Rumble

On June 18, the rivals met again at Fatal 4-Way in Uniondale, New York. Theodore Long had been ordered by Vince McMahon, at McIntyre's request, to watch the match ringside. That demand would end up benefiting

ASK KOFI (based on various interviews)

Q. It's all staged, right?

A. Yes it's staged. However, some of it is improvised. Also, even if getting hit by a chair, falling from a ladder, and jumping/being jumped on from the ropes is scripted, it still really hurts! You may not feel it at the time because of adrenaline, but afterward, you feel it.

Q. Do you take the feuds personally?

A. Respect is big in wrestling. It's an honor to have a feud with a guy like Randy Orton. That being said, you want to win against him!

Q. How important is the crowd?

A. Very important. The crowd has to love you . . . or love to hate you. They have to cheer loudly or boo loudly when you come out. If they don't care, you're in trouble.

Kofi. Both McIntyre and Kofi came close to a pin several times. McIntyre even argued with the referee once, saying that Kofi had been down for three seconds. The referee disagreed. Eventually, the acrobatic Kofi had his legs locked around McIntyre's head, while Kofi's hands were on the ropes. McIntyre, trying to push Kofi off of him, knocked out the referee with Kofi's legs.

Moments later, McIntyre knocked Kofi out—and pinned him—but there was no referee to count! After unsuccessfully trying to waken the sleeping referee, McIntyre grabbed Long and threw him in the ring. Next, McIntyre stripped the shirt off the referee and made Long wear it. Now, Long approached the still-unconscious Kofi. Long counted to two—but refused to say three. That's when Matt Hardy, wearing street clothes, stormed the ring. He quickly tackled McIntyre and then fled. This gave Kofi time to recover. Kofi dealt a dumbstruck McIntyre Trouble in Paradise and then pinned him. This time, Long counted all the way to three!

The feud continued on October 15 in the qualifying match for the final spot on Team SmackDown at Bragging Rights. If he won, Kofi would be a headliner in the type of pay-for-view event he had always hoped to watch as a kid. In a quick match, Kofi pinned McIntyre using Trouble in Paradise. He won and joined a team of seven led by Big Show. Team SmackDown would go on to win against Raw.

Kofi's star was rising. In January 2011, he appeared on the cover of the video game *WWE All-Stars*. It was a thrill for Kofi both as an avid gamer and because he was featured with wrestling legends, including Hulk Hogan, Macho Man, Ultimate Warrior, the Rock, and Randy Orton. Kofi has said that the fun thing about being in a video game like this is that he can play against late greats that have since retired. (On the

Because of his acrobatic style and happy-go-lucky attitud favorite among young wrestling fans. Here, he attends a celebrating WrestleMania XXV.

road, he plays video games against guys he still wrestles today, such as Big Show, Cody Rhodes, and Tyler Rex.)

On January 30, Kofi returned home to Boston for Royal Rumble. He would soon be competing for the chance to headline WrestleMania, known as the Show of Shows. But first, he visited his family. His mother, now a doctor of anthropology, lives in a duplex with Kofi's brother Kwame and sister Kiya. Kwame and Kofi still wrestle when they see each other, just as they did as kids. Kofi's mother is proud of him for making a living doing what he loves to do. At the beauty shop, women ask if she worries that he'll get hurt. She tells them that she is too busy cheering for him to think about that.

While home, Kofi works out every day. But he's not a complete health nut. He always makes time to eat at his favorite Mexican restaurant. He believes that eating lots of meat will help him to maintain his muscular build, which is good because he really likes burgers and burritos!

The night of the event, Kofi entered TD Garden, where the Celtics now play. It was an exciting night for Kofi, a lifelong Celtics fan. He talked to fans outside, tested the *WWE All-Stars* video game, and tweeted to his

A WORD TO THE WISE

Wrestling is a staged and rehearsed event. Wrestlers practice for hours to make their moves look real without actually hurting each other. However, they still often get hurt. Doing the things you read about—or even pretending to do them—could result in serious injury. As the wrestlers say before every show: don't try this at home.

fans. (His fans are called the Boom Squad, and he tweets under the name TrueKofi.) Sadly, Kofi was defeated in front of his family by his longtime nemesis, Orton. He was disappointed but hopeful for the future.

He says he'd like to face more childhood heroes in the ring, such as Ricky "the Dragon" Steamboat. He told ESPN's *The Life* in 2011, "It could be like a student versus teacher type match. For me, being in the same ring as the guys I watched growing up just means so much and that would be amazing to me if I got that chance." He says he may even like to return to his earlier heel roots. Whatever he does, Kofi's old high school wrestling work ethic holds true. He told ESPN, "I like to say, 'If you're not getting better, you're getting worse.'" There is no doubt that fans would see whatever Kofi wanted to dish out.

TIMELINE

1920s Once similar to a boxing competition, pro wrestling becomes a scripted sport.

1930s Needing to fill arenas during the Great Depression, wrestling develops the circuslike atmosphere seen today.

1950s Local wrestling events are broadcast on television. This was a way to draw fans to the arena.

1979 Georgia Championship Wrestling broadcasts the first national wrestling program on TBS.

1980s WWF (which would become WWE) buys local wrestling promotions or acquires their wrestlers to become the largest wrestling promotion. It gears its nationwide television broadcast toward children, with characters like Hulk Hogan and Andre the Giant.

1981 On August 14, Kofi is born in Ghana, West Africa. Soon after, his family moves to America.

Late 1990s Kofi wrestles for Winchester High School.

Early 2000s Kofi graduates from Boston College and joins corporate America.

2005 Kofi begins training at Killer Kowalski's Pro Wrestling School.

2006 Kofi is drafted to the WWE Development Federation.

2007 Kofi's promo videos begin airing during ECW events on the SyFy Channel.

2008 On January 22, Kofi has his pro wrestling television debut.

2008 In April, Kofi is drafted to Raw.

2008 On June 29, Kofi battles Chris Jericho in his first Raw appearance.

2009 On October 25, Kofi interferes with a WWE Championship Match between Randy Orton and John Cena. Orton blames Kofi and a rivalry begins.

2009 On November 16, the feud between Orton and Kofi comes to a head when Orton kicks Rowdy Roddy Piper. Kofi storms the stage and takes Orton down.

2010 On March 28, Kofi dazzles fans during the SmackDown Money in the Bank Ladder Match by using a broken ladder as stilts.

2010 On April 26, Kofi is drafted to SmackDown.

2010 On October 15, Kofi beats his new rival, Drew McIntyre, for a chance to appear on SmackDown's Bragging Rights, a pay-per-view event.

2011 In January, Kofi appears on the cover of the video game *WWE All-Stars*.

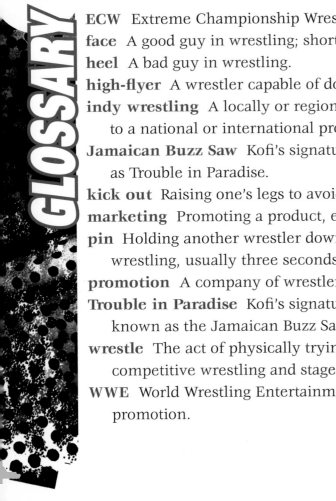

GLOSSARY

ECW Extreme Championship Wrestling, a former WWE brand.

face A good guy in wrestling; short for "baby face."

heel A bad guy in wrestling.

high-flyer A wrestler capable of doing aerial-moves.

indy wrestling A locally or regionally owned promotion, as opposed to a national or international promotion.

Jamaican Buzz Saw Kofi's signature roundhouse kick, now known as Trouble in Paradise.

kick out Raising one's legs to avoid a pin.

marketing Promoting a product, event, or service.

pin Holding another wrestler down for a set amount of time—in pro wrestling, usually three seconds.

promotion A company of wrestlers that stages events.

Trouble in Paradise Kofi's signature roundhouse kick, formerly known as the Jamaican Buzz Saw.

wrestle The act of physically trying to pin another person. There is competitive wrestling and staged wrestling.

WWE World Wrestling Entertainment, a large, international wrestling promotion.

Canadian Wrestling Federation

P.O. Box 51004

Winnipeg, MB R2X 3B0

Canada

(204) 988-4986

Web site: http://www.cwfwrestling.com

Canadian Wrestling Federation is a family oriented, all aboriginal professional wrestling organization.

Chaotic Wrestling/Killer Kowalski Pro Wrestling School

100 Belmont Street

North Andover, MA 01845

(978) 852-8534

Web site: http://www.chaoticwrestling.com

Chaotic Wrestling is an indy wrestling promotion in Boston and home of the Killer Kowalski Pro Wrestling School.

National Guard Youth ChalleNGe

Office of Athletics and Youth Development

Jefferson Plaza 1

Room 2456

1411 Jefferson Davis Highway

Arlington, VA 22202-3231

Web site: http://www.ngycp.org

National Guard Youth ChalleNGe is a program for high school dropouts that teaches life skills and self-discipline. Kofi Kingston is a celebrity spokesperson for this group.

Ohio Valley Wrestling and Training

4400 Shepherdsville Road

Louisville, KY 40218

Web site: http://www.ovwrestling.com

Ohio Valley Wrestling and Training is an indy wrestling promotion and school where many wrestlers get their start.

Ring of Honor Wrestling

P.O. Box 1127

Bristol, PA 19007

(215) 781-2500

Web site: http://www.rohwrestling.com

Ring of Honor is a large indy wrestling promotion.

Total Nonstop Action Wrestling

209 10th Avenue South, Suite 302

Nashville, TN 37203

Web site: http://www.tnawrestling.com

Total Nonstop Action Wrestling is a national promotion televised on Spike T.V.

World Wrestling Entertainment (WWE)

Corporate Headquarters

1241 East Main Street

Stamford, CT 06902

(203) 352-8600

Web site: http://www.wwe.com

WWE is an international wrestling promotion televised throughout the world.

Wrestlemania Reading Challenge

YALSA

50 E. Huron Street

Chicago, IL 60611

Web site: http://www.ala.org/ala/mgrps/divs/yalsa/teenreading/
     wrmc/wrmc.cfm

WrestleMania Reading Challenge is a quiz contest through which kids can win tickets to WrestleMania.

Wrestling Lutte Canada

7-5370 Canotek Road
Ottawa, ON K1J 9E6
Canada
(613) 748-5686
Web site: http://www.wrestling.ca
Wrestling Lutte Canada is an organization for Canadian Olympic-style wrestling.

Web Sites

Due to the changing nature of Internet links, Rosen Publishing has developed an online list of Web sites related to the subject of this book. This site is updated regularly. Please use this link to access the list:

http://www.rosenlinks.com/slam/kk

Black, Jake. *The Ultimate Guide to WWE*. New York, NY: Grosset & Dunlap, 2011.

Kaelberer, Angie Peterson. *The Fabulous, Freaky, Unusual History of Pro Wrestling* (Unusual Histories.) Mankato, MN: Capstone, 2010.

Kreidler, Mark. *Four Days to Glory: Wrestling with the Soul of the American Heartland*. New York, NY: Harper Collins, 2007.

Martino, Alfred. *Pinned*. Boston, MA: Harcourt, 2005.

McIntosh, J. S. *Wrestling* (Getting the Edge: Conditioning, Injuries, and Legal & Illicit Drugs). Broomall, PA.: Mason Crest, 2010.

Sweeney, Joyce. *Headlock*. New York, NY: Henry Holt, 2006.

Beekman, Scott. *Ringside: A History of Professional Wrestling in America*. Westport, CT: Greenwood Publishers, 2006.

Bergeron, Chris. "Wrestle Mania." *Milford Daily News,* August 16, 2006. Retrieved February 6, 2011 (http://www.milforddailynews.com/entertainment/arts/x602864320).

Carraggi, Mike. "Winchester Star Reborn." *Boston Globe*, September 26, 2009 (http://www.boston.com/sports/schools/articles/2009/09/26/winchester_star_reborn).

Encarnacao, Jack. "WWE Star Kofi Kingston Returns to Mass. to Headline Cohasset Show." *Patriot Ledger*, August 26, 2010. Retrieved February 8, 2011 (http://www.patriotledger.com/features/x2143022256/WWE-star-Kofi-Kingston-returns-to-Mass-to-headline-Cohasset-show).

Glazer, Aaron. "Kofi Kingston's WWE Raw Push Is Perfect." Examiner.com, November 24, 2009. Retrieved February 3, 2011 (http://www.examiner.com/pro-wrestling-in-new-york/kofi-kingston-s-wwe-raw-push-is-perfect).

Goffe, Leslie. "Sport: Smackdown." Focus on Africa, July 2, 2008. Retrieved February 6, 2011 (http://www.bbc.co.uk/worldservice/africa/features/focus_magazine/news/story/2008/07/080702_ghana_wrestler.shtml).

Kendall, Justin. "WWE's Kofi Kingston Talks Jumping off Ladders and Avoiding the Undertaker." The Pitch, July 16, 2010. Retrieved February 8, 2011 (http://blogs.pitch.com/plog/2010/07/wwe_kofi_kingston_money_in_the_bank.php).

Kingston, Kofi. "My Life." WWE Kids. Retrieved February 2, 2011 (http://www.wwekids.com/superstars/kofikingston).

Kofi-Kingston.com. "Biography." www.kofi-kingston.com. Retrieved February 2, 2011 (http://www.kofi-kingston.com/biography.html).

Medalis, Kara. "Results: Kingston Takes McIntyre to the Limits." WWE, May 23, 2010. Retrieved February 22, 2010 (http://www.wwe.com/shows/wweoverthelimit/matches/14443544/results).

Murray, Jawn. "King of the Ring: WWE Star Kofi Kingston." Black Voices Buzz, September 15, 2009. Retrieved March 1, 2011 (http://www.bvbuzz.com/2009/09/15/wwe-star-kofi-kingston).

Online World of Wrestling. "Wrestler Profiles." Retrieved February 2, 2011 (http://www.onlineworldofwrestling.com/profiles/k/kofi-kingston.html).

Robinson, Jon. "Kofi Kingston Talks 'WWE All-Stars,' Randy Orton, and Wrestlemania." ESPN the Life, January 31, 2010. Retrieved February 6, 2011 (http://espn.go.com/espn/thelife/videogames/blog/_/name/thegamer/id/6077306/kofi-kingston-talks-wwe-all-stars-randy-orton-wrestlemania).

Sheehan, Nancy. "Kofi's Got His Boom Drop Ready." *Telegram & Gazette*, June 25, 2010. Retrieved February 8, 2011 (http://www.telegram.com/article/20100625/NEWS/6250513/1011).

Shields, Brian, and Kevin Sullivan. *W Encyclopedia: The Definitive Guide to World Wrestling Entertainment*. Indianapolis, IN: DK/Brady Games, 2009.

Tello, Craig. "Rumble Day Diary: Kofi Kingston." WWE.com, January 31, 2011. Retrieved February 8, 2011 (http://www.wwe.com/shows/royalrumble/diary).

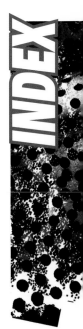

About the Author

Bridget Heos has written numerous books for teens and young adults. She lives in Kansas City, MO, with her husband and three sons.

Photo Credits

Cover, pp. 1, 34–35 Charley Gallay Wirelmage/Getty Images; cover (background photo), p. 1 (background photo), pp. 4–5 Don Arnold/WireImage/Getty Images; p. 3 (boxing ring), chapter openers graphic (boxing ring) © www.istockphoto.com/Urs Siedentop; pp. 8–9 William F. Campbell/Time & Life Images/Getty Images; p. 10 New York Daily News Archive/New York Daily News/Getty Images; p. 13 B. Bennett/Getty Images; pp. 16, 28 Bill Olive/Getty Images; pp. 18–19 Paanoramic/ Imago/Icon SMI; p. 20 © AP Images; p. 23 George Napolitano/FilmMagic/Getty Images; p. 26 Jam Media/ LatinContent Editorial/Getty Images; p. 31 Zuma Press/ Icon SMI; cover background graphic, back cover background graphic, chapter openers background graphic, interior graphics Shutterstock

Designer: Les Kanturek; Editor: Bethany Bryan;
Photo Researcher: Marty Levick